Dear Parents:

This Guide Book is designed for your child to themselves as they draw, read, write, reflect and explore all the ways they can stay connected to their wholeness. I have used metaphors of earth, tree and leaves to help them facilitate that journey.

The psychological and scientific foundations of this book come from: Eco-psychology, Neuroscience, Environmental Stewardship, Somatics and Resilience, Meditation and Mindfulness, Positive Psychology, Non-Violent Communication and Hoffman Quadrinity Process.

Included are many fun activities: art, drawing, visioning, reading, poetry, songs and more. Each is designed to affirm their unique gifts, help them honor their bodies, heart and mind so they can find balance, stay connected to their heart and expand their resilience as they journey through life.

By reading and completing the exercises they will also learn valuable life skills that will nourish them throughout their journey: validation, forgiveness, compassion, gratitude, health, naming and accepting feelings and sensations, releasing feelings, boundary setting, visioning, honoring their wholeness and the wholeness of others.

The gift of remembering who they are awaits them as they learn to ground in the strength of their uniqueness, follow their inner guidance and reach their strong branches out to the places they want to grow into so they become all that they dream of and shine their unique light in the world!

My hope is that all children will grow to BE who they were meant to BE. As Mark Twain put is so eloquently, "The two most important days are the day you were born and the day you find out why." I'm envisioning a world where every child knows why they came to the earth and shares their unique contribution right from the start. Thank you for supporting their journey!   ~ Linda

Luna Madre™ Publishing
3463 State Street, Suite 225
Santa Barbara CA 93105
www.LunaMadre.com

Printed in the United States. Luna Madre Publishing.
www.GrowingUpWhole.com

Growing Up Whole™ A Child's Guide Book
Library of Congress Cataloging-in-Publication Data LCN Number: 2014943981
ISBN: 978-0-9887724-8-9

Editor: Annie J. Dahlgren
Illustrations: Linda Newlin
Graphic Design: Cecilia Martini Muth, CC Design, Santa Barbara CA

For all the children in the world:

May you always remember

WHO YOU TRULY ARE

And that

YOU ARE WHOLE

and as you grow remember that

YOU ARE THE AUTHOR OF YOUR LIFE.

This is your Book

A Guide Book to awaken your awareness and validate your uniqueness and your wholeness so you can live the life you came here to live and give your unique gifts and talents.

It is a journey through activities, artwork, reading, writing, songs and adventures designed to give you life skills to support your life's journey.

You can write anywhere you wish on these pages so grab your crayons, your favorite markers or pencils.

Make it **unique** just like you!

We hope you have FUN learning more about

Who You Are

and

that you will always Shine Your Light

and

BE THE ONE and ONLY YOU

through all the seasons

of your life.

When were you born?

This is the miraculous day of your birth! Your parents were so happy☺!

Write your name here in your favorite colors

Where on the earth were you born?

_____

What season was it?

_____

Draw a picture of your home where you live:

List your favorite things about the place where you get to "grow" up:

You
are part of
the
Earth's Energy

We Need the Earth

We need the AIR to breathe

We need the RAIN to grow all living things

We need the EARTH to sustain us

We need the SUN to give us light

Color the Air, Rain, Earth and Sun

EXERCISE:

Go outside or sit
where you can see the sun.

Take time to experience the peace and
strength that the sun offers to you.

Breathe in the sun's light and feel the
warmth within you.

Feel the energy of the sun inside your
body and let the good feelings run through
all of you.

Name the feelings that you feel in the sun:

Draw a picture of the sun filling you with light:

We grow like trees grow, in rich soil with lots of:

Circle the ones that YOU NEED
to grow and be strong:

Clean Air   Water   Sun

         Kindness   Joy&Laughter

     Love   Support   Peace

Friends   Family   Space&Time to Play

   Nourishing Food   Safety   Rest

The Earth is My Home

Go outside in nature.

Let your self walk around and find a favorite spot.

Become still and listen.

18

What do you hear, smell, see?

What do you notice happening inside you
when you connect with the earth?

Circle things you know about how the earth is:

Life giving   Peaceful   Green

Soft   Kind   Strong

Grounded   Warm   Safe   Windy

Wet   Dry   Hot

Colorful   Beautiful   BIG   Fun

Breezy   Magical

The Earth Needs Us

The earth is a living being just like you are.
What are some things you can do to help
<u>keep the earth strong and healthy?</u>

(some things other children are doing around the world include:
recycling, picking up trash, not using paper products, riding their
bikes, walking, planting trees and conserving water).

Your Body
Is the Home
of
Your Spirit ♡

My Body is the Home of My Spirit♡

I help my body to grow
big and strong

by giving it healthy food
play and rest

stretching and meditation
sleep and water

loving kindness and friendship
gratitude and sunlight

Circle the things you feed your body to grow:

Vegetables   Water   Fresh Fruit

Meat   Fish   Eggs   Dairy

Soy   Nuts   Seeds

Grains   Green Drinks   Vitamins

Other things I do to stay strong and healthy:

Circle the Ones that You Do:

Run and Play Ball   Stretch

Ride Horses   Gymnastics   Ski   Swim

Hike   Sled   Play Chase/Freeze Tag

Ride Bikes   Walk My Dog   Sleep

Yoga   Meditate   Brush Teeth   Dance

Take Vitamins   Rest   Be With Friends/Family

My body grows each year like a tree does.

If I were a tree, this is the kind of tree I would be.

Draw, paint or sketch it here:

You can make your
own growth wall chart
to measure how tall
you are

This unique growth wall chart is available at
GrowingUpWhole.com

A five year old told this story to his
classmates about

The Big Bang Theory

"Once upon a time there was the SUN.

One day there was a big bang
and the sun exploded
into millions of pieces.

That is how the
got into
each and every one of us."

You Are Of The

Within everyone there is the

We call it our Essence or Spirit.

It is eternal.

It is our ♡

BEST SELF.

It leads us to wholeness, joy, peace
and right action.

Some qualities of Your Essence/Spirit

Circle the ones that describe your Spirit

Caring   Kind   Loving   Thoughtful   Alive

Curious   Brave   Strong   Calm   Clear

Patient   Sharing   Real/No Pretending

Just ME   Creative   Trusting   Open

Centered   Accepting   Open   Forgiving

Compassionate   Peaceful   Confident   Lovable

Wise   My Best Self   Self-Directed   Just Knows

Grounded   Intuitive   Connected   Honest

Draw a picture of your BEST SELF

VALIDATE
And
CELEBRATE
YOUR GIFTS !

Your body thrives when you validate
and celebrate YOU and YOUR GIFTS.

Things I like about Myself:

Be sure to include your talents and gifts ♡

Who I Am

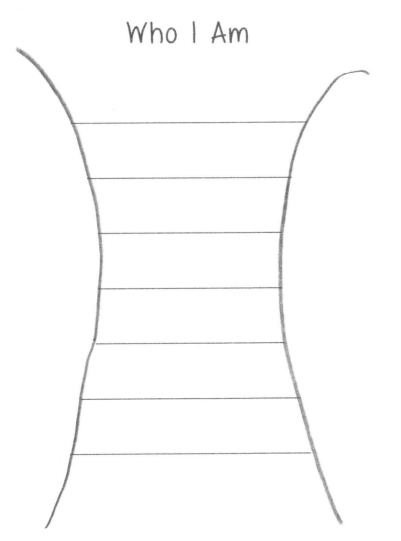

It is a gift you give your self to keep a
list of things that you like about your self
and that others like about you.

People will come and go in your life and many
will tell you what they like about you.

It's good to write it down so when you need
a reminder of who you are
you can read your lists.

This is called **Validation**.

What others like about me:

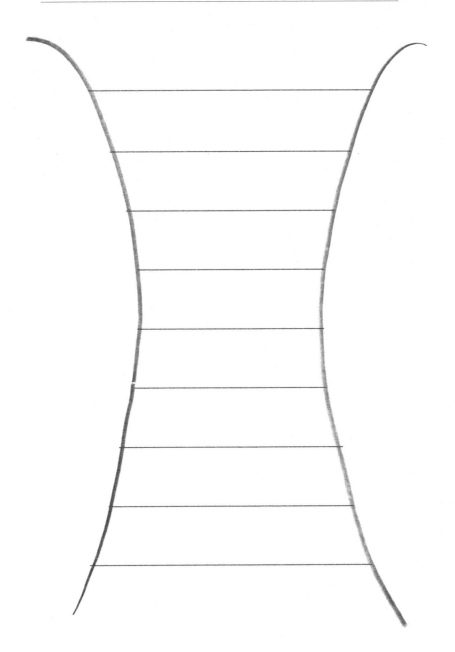

Read the lists you just wrote out loud

♥see page 35 & 37

Allow the positive energy to fill your body as you read the things you like about your self
and
the things others like about you.

Notice how it feels to say these out loud.

Validation is a loving practice for yourself and everyone!

Now practice Validating others.

Tell them what you like about them.

Validation nourishes
our wholeness
and our
knowing

When Something Inside You

Just Knows...

This is Your

Intuition

Your

Inner Wisdom

Intuition

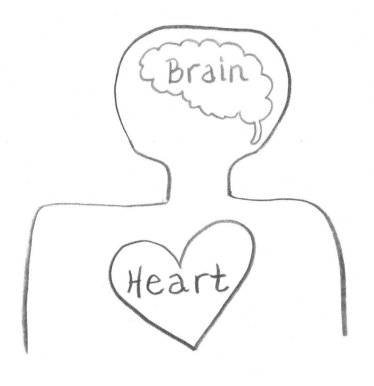

Your Mind
Knows Things

Your Heart
Has Wisdom

Your Gut Feelings
Give Answers

41

LISTENING to your self is very important.

When you listen to your self you learn to trust what you know to be true about you and your experience.

One way we learn to listen to ourselves is to be still and get centered.

This is often called Meditation.

Some call it a Centering Practice.

Centering Practice/Meditation:

Sit or stand still.

Breathe in and out.

Feel your whole body become present.

Listen as you allow your body to speak.

♥ Doctors say having a stillness practice and asking for inner guidance
will help to keep you healthy and connected to your vision/purpose.

You can ask your body
anything you wish to know.

You might ask what your body needs
to heal if you're sick.

You can ask where to look for
something you've lost.

You can ask for what to say
to your friend who's hurt.

You can find peace in the stillness.

When I listen to my heart♡

I will know my truth
and the right actions to take

I will know Who I AM

and what my purpose is for being

and what gifts I have to share
with the world.

"Your vision
will become clear
only when you can look
into your own heart.

Those who look outside,
dream;

Those who look inside;
awaken!"

~Carl Jung

Follow
Your Inner
Guidance

If you follow someone else's compass

it will take you somewhere

other than where you

were meant to go.

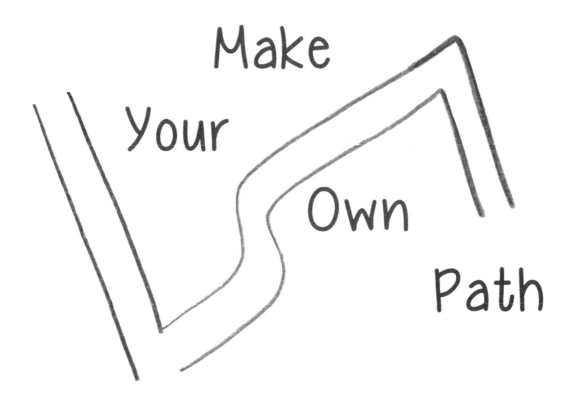

Make

Your

Own

Path

There is NO ONE else exactly like YOU.

Every human being is a unique individual.

No one has the same fingerprint.

And just like snowflakes,

You are ONE of a kind.

Be
Who You Are
and
Reach for
the Stars

DISCOVER

YOUR

PASSIONS

When you do
what you LOVE
you feel good inside.

These are
your PASSIONS.

Circle the things you love to Play and Do:

Soccer Baseball Skipping Hide and Seek Hiking Reading

Jumping Rope Running Fast Riding Bikes Camping

Writing Stories Basketball Swimming Playing Piano

Guitar Drums Petting my Dog Playing with Friends

Tennis Bowling Canoeing Painting Science Writing

Making Music Twirling Cooking/Baking Making Things

Arts/Crafts Skateboarding Playing Make Believe Fishing

Dolls Cars/Trucks Dress Up Skating Skiing

Sailing Drawing Look at Clouds/Stars Carving Wood

Building Forts Gardening Building Legos

These Are Your Passions

Your Passions Are Like Branches of Your Tree

Sample of Johnny's Passion Tree

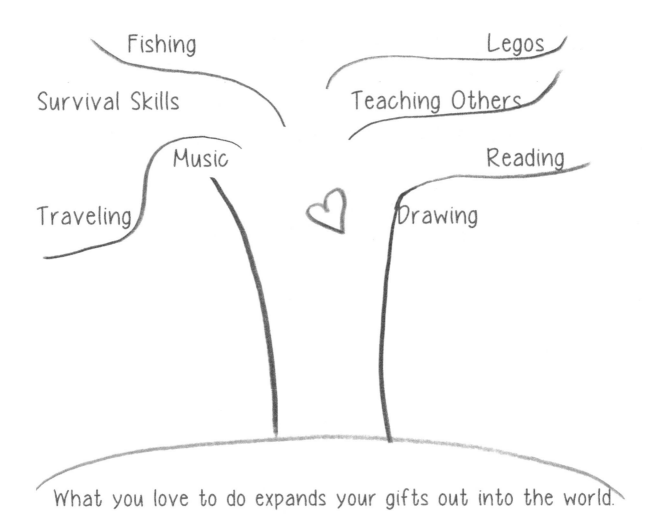

Fishing

Legos

Survival Skills

Teaching Others

Music

Reading

Traveling

Drawing

What you love to do expands your gifts out into the world.

Draw your Passion Tree

You may have many branches of passions or you may have a few branches of things you love to do.

Remember each one of us is unique
so your passion tree may be
different from others'.

The adventure of life is
growing into your favorite passions
and trying on new ones.

You can reach and "branch" out toward
the passions and gifts you want to
experience and express.

When I do my passions, I feel:

HAPPY

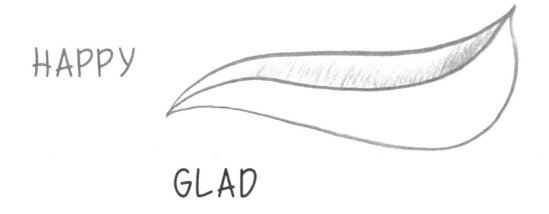

GLAD

EXCITED

ALIVE

What else do you feel inside your body
when you are doing your passions?

When you do what you love you can feel
light, tingly, peaceful, relaxed and
time goes by quickly.

This is called "being in the FLOW."

Choosing to do what we love give us
energy and JOY.

These are called SENSATIONS.

You feel sensations within your body.

Sometimes they feel good,
sometimes they feel neutral
and sometimes they feel uncomfortable.

When you follow your good sensations
you know you love what you are doing.

As you grow and do what you love your
branches grow into areas where your energy
leads you.

Sensations are another guide for your
journey.

Think of a time you were doing something new.

Remember how your body felt inside.

Did you feel sweaty, tingly, numb, cold, hot or was your heart thumping?

When you do something new it can sometimes feel uncomfortable at first.

These SENSATIONS inform of us of what is going on inside us at that moment.

It is energy that moves in and out of us.

More Sensations

Tingly   Shaky   Scared   Dry   Excited

Butterflies in tummy   Light   Tense

Relieved   Hot   Cold   Hopeful

Tickled   Safe   Cozy   Numb

Strong   Hungry   Tired   Itchy

Sometimes your sensations tell you to

MOVE AWAY

from something or someone.

This is important information.

Please listen to your body.

Your body doesn't lie.

Your body will tell you if you need to set a boundary and say "NO" to whatever or whoever is not good for you.

Having a healthy NO is very important.

Practice saying NO.

You decide WHO you want to invite into your circle.

Choose by listening to your sensations.

Boundary Setting Practice

The Rope Circle

Take a rope or string and make a circle around you on the floor. You are in the middle of the circle. The area between you and the rope circle is your personal space. You're in the center. You can make your circle as big as you like.

Imagine someone wants to enter into your circle. You can practice saying "No" "Not now" or "Yes come into my circle."

Your circle may be small some days or larger on other days. You may want a few people near or many people close to you.

You have permission to practice sensing when you want to say NO and use your voice to express your truth of how you feel at that time.

Rope Circle

When you have
a healthy

NO
~~~~~~~~~~

You will have
a healthy

YES
~~~~~~~~

Remember to listen
to your
body's sensations
and trust
your intuition.

They will guide you
throughout your life.

It is Natural to Feel All of My Feelings

69

Emotions Are Like Leaves.

Emotions are energy.

Emotions move and change.

Emotions are Messengers.

Emotions give me important information.

I can have many feelings at once.

All of my feelings are a natural part
of being human.

Sometimes I feel happy

Sometimes I feel sad

Sometimes I feel silly

Sometimes I feel bad

Sometimes I feel excited

Sometimes I feel mad

Emotions are Messengers.

When you feel mad it is letting you know that something just happened that is NOT OK!

Think about the last time you were angry. Remember what happened that wasn't OK.

Anger is like all emotions. It is ENERGY that needs to move out of you and it is telling you how you feel about something that has happened.

Releasing your feelings is an important practice so you can be healthy and peaceful.

Healthy ways to release feelings:

When you are sad crying can help release the pain.

When you are mad you can express and release anger/frustration in various ways:

You can talk to someone about it.

You can hit a foam bat on a pillow to vent the frustration and anger safely without hurting anyone (especially your self).

You can write an anger letter and tear it up.

Letting your feelings flow
is important because

feelings that get stuck inside
can make you sick.

Scientists have discovered that tears help to
release from our body a stress hormone
(called Cortisol) which means crying is key to
staying healthy and reducing stress.

My body needs to express
what I am feeling

and

my body is designed
to release all of my emotions naturally.

Write/name some feelings you have felt in the leaves below:

Crying is good for ME

So is Laughing Myself Silly

☮

I'm going to let all of my feelings

flow

Your Feelings often give you clues to what you need.

Draw or list the things you need:

I asked MacKenzie age 6 what she needs most?
She drew this picture of kindness

Communicating My Needs In A Kind Clear Way Is A Practice

Naming my NEEDS and making REQUESTS

One way to communicate my needs clearly and kindly is to say:

"Would you be willing to...?

(give me my toy back now)?"

If they say "no" you could say

"When would you be willing to...?

(give it back to me)?"

They will likely negotiate a time
to give it back.

If you can wait for that time period
then all is well.

However, if they say "later" or "not ever"
then you can express your specific need.

"I understand you don't want to give it
back to me now but I need to have
my toy back in 5 minutes
because I'm leaving the park
and I have to take it home with me."

When we use language like

"Are you Willing?"

We invite others to hear our request and not feel that we are being demanding.

"I am feeling..."

"I need..."

"I would like to spend time with you."

"Would you be willing to read and snuggle with me now?"

Listening to others
and
allowing them to
communicate their needs
is important, too.

This is how you can learn to
understand
and see where they are coming from
and what is true for them.

Be Curious!

When people ask you,
"What do you want to be
when you grow up?"

You might say

"The Best ME
I Can Be."

My Future = Who I Want to Be

"The two most important days are...

The day you were born

and

The day you find out

WHY

YOU were born"

~Mark Twain

Honor Your
Hopes
And
Your Dreams

"Dream no small dream
for they have no power to move
the hearts of men."

~ Goethe

"The future belongs to those who believe
in the beauty of their dreams."

~ Eleanor Roosevelt

"Some men see things as they are
and ask why?

Others dream things that never were
and ask why not?"

~ George Bernard Shaw

Having dreams
is part of living whole.

Your dreams often reveal
what you truly want.

I dream about:

"Your imagination is a preview
of life's coming attractions."

- Albert Einstein

When you believe...

Magic can happen.

If You Believe 🎵

If you believe, within your heart you'll know

That no one can change, the path that you must go

Believe that you can go home, believe you can float on air

Then click your heels 3 times, If you believe, then you'll be there

Believe in your Self right from the start

Believe in the magic that's inside your heart

Believe all these things not because I told you to

But believe in your Self, just believe in your Self

Just believe in your Self as I believe in you

Believe there's a reason to be

Believe you can float on air

And know from the moment you try

If you believe, then you'll be there

Believe in your Self, right from the start

And you'll have a brain and you'll have a heart

And you'll have the courage to last your whole life through

But believe in your Self, If you believe in your Self

Just believe in your Self, as I believe in You!

"Go confidently
in the direction
of your dreams.

Live the life
you have imagined."

~ Harry David Thoreau

VISIONING as a Practice

Visioning helps create your life the way
you want it to be.

Imagine how you want your day to go.

See your self moving through the day exactly
as you desire it to be.

Feel the sensations of how it will feel.

Choose this vision for your self.

Visioning can be used in all areas of life.

Visualize your self playing the piano well.

Visualize making the basketball go into the hoop.

Visualize passing your spelling test.

Visualize your body healing any illness you have.

Make a Vision Board

Putting your vision onto paper is called a Vision Board.

You can take magazine pictures you cut out or words or draw/paint your own images on a big poster board.

Paste or draw/paint your vision just as you want it.

An example:

If you wanted to visit the snow and spend your birthday at Lego Land you would cut out pictures of snow places where people were doing what you wanted to do and find pictures of the Lego Land hotel and paste them on the vision board.

It becomes a visual reminder of your heart's desires.

You can put anything on it. (health, peace, love, joy, friends)

Watch and see how your visions come true.

My Vision:

Make
Wishes

Making lists and drawing pictures of what
you wish for helps you stay connected
to what you want

and connected to all POSSIBILITIES.

IT's FUN to wish for anything and everything
your heart desires. ♡

You may not always get everything
you wish for,

but having wishes, hopes and dreams
makes life magical.

Make WISH LISTS

You can make them anytime of year...

What I want for my next BIRTHDAY!

Make a list or draw pictures of what you are wishing for:

What I want for the HOLIDAYS!

Make a list or draw pictures of what you want

Include: Gifts and Feelings and Experiences you want to have:

What I wish for the world and others to have:

Treasure
Your
IMAGINATION

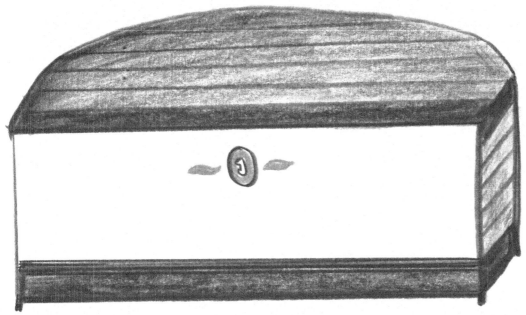

"If you can imagine it,
you can achieve it.

If you can dream it,
you can become it."

~ William Arthur Ward

Honor
and cherish
your
CREATIVITY

Circle the ways you like to create:

Drawing   Painting   Clay/Ceramics Wood working

Crocheting   Needlework   Weaving Cut outs   Knitting

Crayons   Markers   Mud Pies   Building   Cooking

Carving Sewing   Writing Stories   Writing songs   Baking

Playing instruments/making music   Beeswax

Playdough   Making up games   Origami Building forts

"I am not afraid of storms,
for I am learning
how to sail
my ship."

~ Louise May Alcott "Little Women"

When Storms Come

My Boat Will Be Ready

Navigate Life
with
Resilience
and
Positive Life Skills

Keep believing in your self.

Especially when things are hard.

Sometimes bad things happen
and you will get hurt.

Sometimes you won't get what you wish for.

Sometimes you will lose.

Sometimes you will fall off.

Sometimes you will mess up.

Hard things will happen.

There is loss and grief.

Sometimes people will mistreat you
and may be mean.

But what is amazing is that you will...

BACK

E

C

B O N C E

O

U

113

Yes

You

Will

Bounce Back!

Because

YOU are BIGGER

than

ANYTHING

That has ever happened to you

and

YOU are RESILIENT!

"You're braver
than you believe. ♡

Stronger than you know
and
Smarter than you think."

~ A.A. Milne "Winnie the Pooh"

When you're feeling down you can bounce back by doing <u>some of these things</u>:

Go out in nature. Take a walk. Connect with the earth.

Draw/Paint/Make something/Express your creativity.

Play or listen to music you like.

Hang out with animals.

Talk to a loving friend or family member.

Volunteer to help others/Give back.

Other things that can help when you are feeling down:

Feel and release all of your emotions.

Have a good cry.

Howl at the moon. ☺

Dance.

Write in your journal.

Remember the truth of who you are.

Remember a time you felt happy before

and

Remind your self "I CAN DO THIS!"

When you say "I CAN"... You CAN.

Try it!

Next time you are doing something new
or something that feels hard

Say to your self
"I CAN"

"The moment you doubt whether you can fly,
you cease forever being able to do it."

~ Peter Pan

What I Say Matters.

The power of my words can make more things possible.

EnCOURAGing words helps us all find our COURAGE.

"I am learning,
I am not failing."

~ Johnny

Persistence Pays
Never Give Up

Remember that Thomas Edison
made 1,000 light bulbs
before he got one that worked
the way he hoped it could.

What if he had stopped at # 394 ?

You may have some very challenging
things to deal with.

Remember your spirit and body are

STRONG

and you can use all your skills, talents,
tools, practices, and resilience
to get through anything and accomplish
all that you dream of.

Remember the first time you did
something really scary and
you did it anyway.

Inside you
is a very
BRAVE YOU

who has already done
amazing things.

Remember to say

"I can do anything!"

WORDS
can heal
and
change the world.

Practice using positive words
that make you and others feel good.

What are your favorite positive words?

Circle the ones you love to hear

You did it!   I love you   Fantastic work

Yes you can   You are cool

Wonderful performance   You worked hard

You can do it   I believe in you   Well done

You've got this   Beautiful creation

You're smart   I like having you as my friend

Remember how good it feels when someone says

"THANK YOU" for your help.

Remember when someone asks

"PLEASE, may I borrow your toys?"

Remember when someone tells you they

LOVE YOU and

how happy they are that you were born.

Remember how it feels when someone says

"WELL DONE! or YOU CAN DO IT!"

When you use positive, encouraging words
to your self and with your friends
wonderful things can happen.

Say nice things to

your family and friends this week.

Notice how it feels to give love in this way.

Notice what good feelings
the other person
feels when you use positive words.

Self Loving Practices

Validation

Installing Happiness

Celebration

Gratitude

Compassion

Forgiveness

Kindness

Shine My Unique Light

A Self-loving Validation Ritual

Share out loud or write down things
you did well:

Notice how good it feels to honor your self in this way
Do it every day if you can.

♥You can buy a Self Validation Journal @ www.GrowingUpWhole.com

Creating More Happiness

You can create happiness within by letting the energy of Self-loving validation soak into your whole body.

When someone gives you a compliment, let it land inside you and fill you up with positive feelings.

When you want to feel good remember what it feels like to be loved and cared about.

Allow those wonderful feelings to SOAK IN to every cell in your body. This is called SAVORING the good feelings.

Scientists call this Installing Happiness.

Our brain wires happiness when it feels positive feelings, so celebrate, validate and do things that make you feel happy.

Celebrate
The JOY of Life!

Circle all the ways you love to celebrate:

Jump Up and Down   Cake and Ice Cream   Sing

Eat My Favorite Dinner Out   Vacation

Mom Cooks Favorite Dinner   Party with Family

Buy/Make Gifts   Dance   Camping

Blow Out Candles   Clap Hands and Cheer

Go on a Trip   Pinatas   Stay up Late   Picnics

Self validation builds your resilience.

Other things that help you feel happy, bounce back and stay balanced are

Compassion **and** Gratitude.

COMPASSION is:

The desire to remove pain and suffering.

Compassion is when your heart feels for someone else's pain and you wish their pain would stop.

You can also have compassion for your self.

When you are hurting you can feel your heart wishing that your own pain would stop.

GRATITUDE is:

Feeling appreciation in your heart and saying "Thank You" and/or writing thank you notes.

WHAT are you thankful for ?

"No act
of kindness,
no matter how small,
is ever wasted."

~ Aesop's Fables

The Lion and the Mouse

WHO are you thankful for ?

Write some thank you notes or say thank you to these
people above and tell them how much you value
their loving support.

My Actions
Affect Other People.

The Golden Rule reminds me to:

Treat others the way
I would like to be treated.

And yet sometimes
people do not act kindly.

Sometimes people will say or do things
that hurt you.

They might do this if they are feeling hurt,
stressed, tired or angry.

It helps to practice letting these things
fly past you and not let them land
in your heart (if possible).

However, sometimes hurtful words
and actions land inside us.

You can release this negative energy.

Energy Release Practice:

When someone's energy or words hurt you
you can SHAKE THEM OFF.

Yes, your body can SHAKE, SHIVER,

SQUIRM and DANCE as you WIGGLE

and GIGGLE your way free

of the icky, sticky sensations.

Try it!

Imagine someone has just said or done
something that hurts.

Now imagine it's a color or a shape of
something sticky.

Let your body shake it off,
squirm and wiggle
and toss it off of you.

Have fun!

When you're all done notice how it feels
to be free of that
Heebie Jeebie negative energy.

FEEL your good feelings
and reinstall happiness.

You can shake off anything

and then...

It's a good time to practice COMPASSION for someone else who may be hurting and wish that their pain would stop.

People can hurt others or put their energy on to others when they are hurting.

It's NOT OK but it happens.

Picture their heart healing
and becoming peaceful
once their pain stops.

Forgiveness is a gift I give
to myself and to others.

We all can say or do things that hurt
others sometimes.

Practice saying "I forgive you"

and

"Please forgive me"

Asking for and giving forgiveness is a precious
gift we give each other and to the world.

When we let go of past hurts we create
peace and a space for good things
to enter into all our lives.

We create freedom for all human beings
to be their best selves and shine
their light in the world.

This is what the world needs,

all people living as their Best Self,

sharing their gifts and making the world
a more peaceful loving place.

I Forgive Myself for:

I Forgive Others for:

It is a Gift I give myself
and the world

To Own my Wholeness

And BE ME

Shining My Unique Light

in the World!

This Little Light of Mine 🎵

This little light of mine, I'm gonna let it shine

This little light of mine, I'm gonna let it shine

This little light of mine, I'm gonna let it shine

Let it shine, let it shine, let it shine

With my heart and soul, I'm gonna let it shine

With my heart and soul, I'm gonna let it shine

With my heart and soul, I'm gonna let it shine

Let it shine, let it shine, let it shine

Everywhere I go, I'm gonna let it shine

Everywhere I go, I'm gonna let it shine

Everywhere I go, I'm gonna let it shine

Let it shine, let it shine, let it shine

Won't let anyone blow it out, I'm gonna let it shine

Won't let anyone blow it out, I'm gonna let it shine

Won't let anyone blow it out, I'm gonna let it shine

Let it shine, let it shine, let it shine

Reminders ♡ For My Journey

It is natural to SHINE MY LIGHT IN THE WORLD.

I am whole and I am complete just as I am now.

Feeling my feelings will help me stay connected to my wholeness, the earth and all living things. I will be healthy, loved, safe and connected.

I am part of my family, school, community and the earth.

I stay balanced, healthy and resilient through life's ups and downs by using my self-loving practices (validation, feeling my feelings, compassion, giving and receiving forgiveness and cherishing my hopes, dreams and wishes.)

My Inner Guidance will take me where
my heart wants to be. ♡

Finding MY life's purpose
and sharing my gifts will bring the greatest joy.

I will BELIEVE in my self and say "I CAN".

It is my birthright to claim my place on the
earth and to grow deep roots, a strong heart,
expansive branches and feel the feelings that
come and go with living life.

I Will Dream Big!

Say "YES" to You!

Yes to your hopes, dreams and wishes!

Yes to Living Whole and Being YOU!

Yes to protecting your earth home!

Yes to World Peace!

Yes to everyone being their Best Self!

We're all part of a circle of life here on earth.

There are billions of people on the planet and each one is unique and brings their own special gifts

YOU are unique and so is everyone else.

We Celebrate You and Everyone's Wholeness

Thank you for cherishing all beings and taking care of the earth you live on.

We dream of a world where all children grow up

knowing who they are and cherishing their gifts and talents,

growing into all areas of their passions,

bouncing back from life's hard moments,

and knowing they are love, loving and lovable

at all times.

Light and Love to you! Linda

Remember...

You are Whole!

And You
Always
Will Be

152

Your heart
is big enough

for everyone
and everything!

Some of Our Favorite Books

All The World by Liz Garton Scanlon

A Life Like Mine: How Children Live Around the World by Unicef and Harry Belafonte

Each Breath a Smile by Thich Nhat Hanh & Sister Susan

I Feel Silly and Other Moods and Where Do Balloons Go? by Jamie Lee Curtis

Kindness by Sarah Conover   Incredible you! by Wayne Dyer

Only One You by Linda Kranz

On The Day You Were Born & No Ordinary Birthday Cake by Debra Frasier

People by Peter Spier   The Greening Book by Ellen Sabin

The Kissing Hand by Audrey Penn

The Nature Connection by Clare Walker Leslie

The Stone by Dianne Hofmeyr and Jude Daly

Tiger-Tiger Is It True? By Byron Katie and Hans Wilhelm

To Everything by Bob Barner   Uno's Garden by Graeme Base

When I Was A Boy I Dreamed By Justin Matott

When I Was A Girl I Dreamed by Margaret Baker

Whoever You Are by Mem Fox

This book is dedicated to my son Johnny

and my God Children Dillon and McKensey

Whom I love with all my ♡

Inspirational gifts available at
GrowingUpWhole.com

Growth Chart
Validation Journals
Music and More

Other Books In Our Collection
Being Whole: A Teen's Guide Book
Living Whole: A Guide Book for Adults
Raising Whole Children: A Parent's Guide Book

♥a portion of all profits go to helping children heal

Peace to you
for your
WHOLE
life's
journey!

☮

Growing Up Whole

A Child's Guide Book

Linda Newlin